Badger's Rugby Compendium

Also By Niall Edworthy

Otto Eckhart's Ordeal

England: The Official FA History
Lord's: The Home of Cricket
The Second Most Important Job in the Country
Jonah Lomu: A Giant Amongst Men

Main Battle Tank
Planet Darts

The Optimist/Pessimist's Handbook

Badger's Cricket Compendium
Badger's Golf Compendium
Badger's Football Slang & Banter

The Curious Gardener's Almanac
The Curious Bird Lover's Almanac
The Curious World of Christmas

Football Stories: Bad Boys & Hard Men
Shit Ground No Fans (as Jack Bremner)

The F**kit! List

Badger's Rugby Compendium

An Illustrated A to Z Glossary of Rugby Terms, Jargon & Slang

Niall Edworthy

Illustrations by Mudd Bexley

Badger Books Ltd, 2025

Copyright © Niall Edworthy 2025

Niall Edworthy asserts the moral right to be identified as the author and compiler of this work

All images © Mudd Bexley

ISBN: 978-1-0685854-8-7

eBook ISBN: 978-1-0685854-9-4

Cover & Book Design: Principal Publishing

Author website: nialledworthy.com

Illustrator: Instagram @izustrations

Egg Chaser – Rugby player or fan

Bum Sniffing – A sceptic's take on rugby

CONTENTS

Author's Note ix
Foreword xi

Aerial Ping-Pong » Attacking Rugby *2*
Back into Traffic » Bury *5*
Camp In » Cuff, Off the *14*
Dark Arts » Dump tackle *23*
Early Pressure » Eye-gouging *29*
Facial » Front Up *32*
Gain Line » Gumshield *38*
Hacking » Helter-Skelter *43*
Ice Bath » Knows the Way to the Try-Line *48*
Latcher » Lump, Big..*53*
Made to Look Silly » Mulligrubber *59*
Nause » Numbers! *64*
Obstruction » Ownership, Taking *68*
Pack » Pylons..*71*
Raking » Running on Empty *78*
Schoolboy Mistakes » Subs Suit *84*
Tackle Suit » Turnstile Defence *93*
Uncontested Scrum » Varsity Match *100*
Wales » Zinzan *104*

Acknowledgements *109*
About the Author...*111*

Author's Note

There are just under 500 words and phrases in this collection, commonly heard in the world of rugby, and some not so commonly, from the changing room, the training ground, the commentator's box, pitch-side, the stands, the pub and the sofa. There are probably another couple of hundred out there, but I hope I have cleared out most of the main ones and the good ones. I hope to update the book with a 2nd edition in the coming years – no doubt more terminology will emerge – and I will slot in any I may have missed this time around.

Most of the entries would be categorised as jargon or slang, the insider's language from a self-contained world. There are a few regular 'official' rugby terms in there too, but I have sought to avoid making this a dull lexicon for the Dummy or Bluffer. I have written it for fans, assumed they have a good feel for the culture of the game and tried to make my definitions amusing as well as enlightening.

Do email me at niall@nialledworthy.com if I have missed any that are worthy of inclusion and I will be sure to include them in the next edition.

Women's rugby is flourishing today, and more power to their elbows. I hope female readers will forgive me for using He/Him pronouns throughout this book. I do that only because switching between 'He' and 'She' makes for a clunky, jarring read.

NE, 2025

Foreword

IF YOU HAD NEVER seen a rugby match, say you were born and bred on Pluto, but you were fluent in English, on tuning into a match, you might ask yourself three questions: i) Why are all these people rolling around in the mud? ii) Why are they so cross with each other? iii) Why is the commentator talking in Klingon?

Many people let rugby pass them by, as they do cricket and other sports built upon a complex set of rules. To understand the rules, to take some pleasure from a sport, as with anything else in life, you must understand the language by which it is described. To go one level deeper and take joy from the sport and immerse yourself in its culture, traditions and nuances, you must have a working knowledge of its jargon and slang. What do they say? The limit of my world is the limit of my words.

'He's hoisted a bomb there, buried him with a snotter, gone in for the jackal, hands all over the egg, given him a facial, and kicked off the handbags. He's getting pinged here, and he's got himself ten minutes riding the pine, or I'm Bill Beaumont.'

There's only one reaction a rugby stranger might have to that: 'You what?' I mean, no wonder the rugby-curious viewer keeps flicking the remote.

The aim of this little glossary of rugby union jargon, banter and vernacular is to offer some light entertainment for the devoted fan, but I hope too that it offers a little enlightenment for the uninitiated and the rugby-curious. If you are Pluto-born and bred, I hope you find this book a helpful introduction to the ancient game loved by millions around our funny little planet and who knows? You might even be eligible to play for Scotland.

Abbreviations

A.k.a. – Also Known As

Arch. – Archaic

Aus. – Australian

Derog. – Derogatory

Dipl. – Diplomatic

Euph. – Euphemism

Fig. – Figurative

S Hem – Southern Hemisphere

N Hem – Northern Hemisphere

A

Aerial Ping-Pong – Tedious battle of the boots when two-full-backs kick the ball to each other, the other players trot back and forth and everyone else groans and nods off. See Also **Kick Tennis**

Against the Head/Feed – *Arch.* Obsolete tradition at the scrum when the defending hooker wins the put-in. This mini-drama vanished in the early 2000s, the emphasis shifting to scrummaging power, the scrumhalf now popping the ball straight into the second row like a waiter bringing drinks

Amateur Spirit – Shaking hands and asking after the family at the bottom of a ruck, then punching and eye-gouging each other five minutes later

Anti-Inflammatories – The rugby player's little helpers

Arm Wrestle – Tight game between two strong teams

Arse, Blowing out of – Shredded, knackered, out of gas, out on the feet

Asking Questions of the Defence – Meaningless way of saying that one side is slightly getting the better of the other

Attack the Outside Shoulder – Pompous way of describing a player trying to run around the man opposite him rather than at him

Attacking Rugby – Broad expression, generally describing a team that is passing the ball and taking risks rather than kicking it and keeping it among the forwards. See also **Ten-Man Rugby**

B

Back into the Traffic – When the ball finally emerges from a melée and the first receiver decides it's a good idea to run straight back into it

Back Row Move – Grand expression for the simple manoeuvre of a Number Eight picking up the ball from the base of the scrum, running two yards and passing it to a flanker

Backed Himself – Commentator's presumption that the player on the ball is super-confident in what he is doing

Backroom Personnel – Guys in trackies with walkie-talkies trying to look useful

Ball and All – Big hit, smothering tackle that prevents the carrier from offloading

Ball on a String – When the fly-half is lacing kicks with the precision of a drone strike

Ball Carrier – The bloke with the ball

Ball Security – Not the heavies on the door at a posh dance but the modern science of holding and protecting the ball properly. Comes with modules in carrying technique, contact awareness, post-tackle protection and support play. See Also **Loose Carry**

Banana Skin, Potential – *Dipl.* Polite way of saying the upcoming opposition is shit

Banquet – Usually an award ceremony in a fancy hotel

(Dorchester) that grows increasingly Medieval as the evening wears on, and the wine is necked, ending in jousting, tabletop theatrics and black-tie wrestling

Banter, Bants – Verbal japes, common to all rugby teams. Often cruel and reductive, banter is a form of affection and a powerful bonding tool. To be a victim of 'Bants' is the proof you belong. If no one ever rips your ego, it's time to find a new club

Baptism of Fire – When the rugby gladiator is sent into the Coliseum for the first time and is mauled to shreds

Basics, Need to Get Back to – When a team is being battered, their best-laid game strategy lies in tatters, and they have absolutely no clue how to deal with the onslaught

Battle-hardened/scarred – i) Of a team that has grown together through adversity towards success or greatness ii) Of a player towards the end of his career, taped up like a mummy and latticed with surgery scars, bloated ears, a crooked nose, a perennial light limp, looking forward to watching the damned game from the comfort of a pub sofa

Beasting Session – Brutal shift on the training ground, borderline abuse that would be illegal if the participants didn't turn up voluntarily

Bench – *Fig.* It's been a long time since substitutes sat on a real wooden bench. More like an ergonomic Imax cinema seat these days

Bench-warmer – Replacement

Big Motor – Of a player with extraordinary stamina and work rate still going strong after 80 minutes when everyone else is on their knees. See Also **Arse, Blowing out of**

Big Stage – When the player steps out from the wings of club rugby into the bright lights of international competition

Bigger they are the Harder they Fall – Total bullshit lie told to terrified little eight-year-olds during their first tackling session

Bill – *S Hem* – Aussie and New Zealand slang for the World Cup, officially the William Webb Ellis Cup

Bin Juice – **Bench-warmers** and second-stringers who can't make the first team but play a useful role as crash-test dummies and banter bait for the big boys

Binding/the Bind – Another obscure area of scrum-maging worthy of a module for students sitting a course in Scrum Law. All three units of the scrum – front row, locks and back row – must 'bind', but refs are only interested in the props, waiting whistle in mouth to **Ping** them if they are holding the wrong part of the shirt or exerting the wrong kind of pressure

Biting – Down there with **Eye-gouging** as the lowest form of skulduggery on the rugby field. A rare but barbaric practice that has virtually disappeared from the game since the introduction of multi-camera television coverage

Blinder – Of a player who has enjoyed a very impressive game

Blindside – The dark alley down the narrow side of the pitch, perfect for a quick getaway but at the risk of a mugging

Blistering Pace – One gear up from **Wheels** or **Gas**. Usually of a winger or full-back. See also **Turbo**

Blitz Defence – Aggressive, high-risk, smothering strategy where whole back line bursts forward and prays no one breaks through into the vast open spaces left behind. See also **Rush Defence**

Blood Bin – Rugby equivalent of a Minor Injuries Unit or Cottage Hospital, without the long wait, where players with cuts go to be bandaged

Bloodbath – The aftermath of an especially brutal contest. See Also **Carnage**

Blood Replacement – A player transfusion where a **Bench-warmer** takes the field while the injured player is treated

Bodies Everywhere – When the field of combat lies strewn with the wounded, the exhausted and the groaning

Body on the Line – When a player sacrifices himself and risks injury in the cause of the team, usually a last-ditch tackle, fighting solo at the **Breakdown**, taking the inevitable big hit in collecting a high ball or running at pace into the defensive line

Bog Snorkelling – A match played in a downpour and swamp

Bomb – A very high kick under which the fullback must show he is worth his place and his salary. See Also **Box Kick; Snow, Coming Down With**

Bomb Squad – Buzz phrase used to describe the powerful unit of forwards brought on by South Africa in the second half, often the entire front row in one exchange

Bottle – To face a challenge but not be equal to it. See Also **Choke**

Bounce of the Ball – Which way will it go? Referring

to the erratic rebound of the egg-shaped **Pill**. Tight contests have been decided by its whimsy

Box Kick – Tedious but effective tactic, to many a blight on the beauty of the game, by which the scrumhalf **Hoists** a high ball to gain ground and in the hope that his team-mates can get the better of the gathering of full-back or wing, regain possession and secure fast ball in a disrupted field. Often leads to the wretched spectacle of an **Aerial Ping Pong** duel

Breadbasket, Right in the – The all-too-common outcome of the **Box Kick** when the opposition player, usually the full-back, takes the high kick cleanly and gratefully, the excitement deflates and the crowd sighs

Breakdown – The crucial short period after the tackle before a ruck or maul is formed and possession is up for grabs

Brick Shithouse – An especially large and formidable player. Common phrase rarely heard on commentary

Brute Strength – Usually in reference to a forward who has battered his way over the line from close range

Building Something Special – Of a coach or a squad of players that has hit a winning streak with the World Cup on the horizon

Bullocking – Always of a forward in possession on

a high-stepping and snorting burst into the enemy lines

Bumface – Nickname for former England captain Will Carling, inspired by the cleft on his chin

Bum Sniffing – A sceptic's take on Rugby

Bury – Heavy tackle that drives the player backwards and inters him in the turf like a corpse

C

Camp, In – When the international squad gathers at a fancy hotel or resort complex ahead of a major tournament for daytime **Beasting**, evening Powerpoint presentations, dodgy videos and Xbox after lights out and maybe a round of golf at the end of the week as a reward for being good boys

Car Crash – Bone-shuddering collision of two players. It has been calculated that a forward in the modern game will suffer the equivalent of about two dozen 30-mph car crashes in the course of a rugby match

Carnage – Brutal contest. See Also **Bloodbath, Bodies Everywhere**

Catch-up Rugby – When fine mathematic calculations are no longer necessary, and a team just needs to score a shitload of points in any way possible

Cattle Truck – Melée situation, usually a maul, where players are tightly packed together like beasts of burden

Caught Napping – When a player has dozed off and the opposition exploit his inattention to make a significant break or score a try

Cauliflower Ear – When the hearing organ has become permanently swollen and deformed and morphs into a hideous slab of indeterminate flesh. Caused by repeated trauma suffered by front forwards in scrummaging, the blood collecting between cartilage and skin

Causing All Sorts of Headaches – Migraine-inducing cliché describing the effect of a playmaker running the game, triggering mild discomfort to intense throbbing in the heads of the fifteen men he is bamboozling

Cavalry Charge – Old-school move at a penalty near the try-line when multiple players start sprinting and the scrumhalf delivers the ball to one of them at full pelt. Considered too dangerous against static tacklers, it is now prohibited under rugby law

Changing the Angles – A switch in the direction of play affected by backs running diagonal lines, variations in passing and kicking into fresh areas of the field

Chasing Shadows – A prop in pursuit of a wing

Cheap Shot – Sly act of foul play, usually a punch away from the action or a stamp at the break-up of a ruck

Cheap Yards – When the ball carrier gains easy territory thanks to ineffective or non-existent tackling. See Also **Real Estate**

Chip – i) A little kick forward ii) Post-match meal at a small provincial club

Choke – i) Failure to deliver when it counts owing to lack of self-belief. See Also **Bottle** ii) Strangle someone at the bottom of a ruck

Choke Tackle – When the tackler keeps the ball carrier on his feet to prevent him from releasing the ball, forcing a maul to form in the hope of a **Turnover** scrum

Chop Tackle – Low, hard and scything, bringing the ball carrier down on the spot. Often deployed in a last effort to prevent a try when an ordinary tackle will be insufficient to arrest the momentum

Class, Pure – Something you just can't teach. It's permanent. Form is temporary

Clean Ball – Scrumhalf's delight. Or surprise. When the ball emerges from the scrum, lineout or ruck smoothly

and quickly, as though handed over by an Amazon deliveryman, allowing the attacking side to sustain momentum and move straight into the next phase

Cleaned Out – The violent but legal removal of opposition players from the **Breakdown** securing fast, **Clean Ball**

Clean Up – i) Tidy the mess of bodies and ball around the ruck for the scrumhalf ii) Put the guy on his arse with a massive tackle

Clothesline – Phrase nicked from Pro wrestling, an illegal high challenge when the tackler flat-arms the man around his neck or head

Coach Killer – A rookie error or poor decision that has the coach reaching into the drawer for the pearl-handled revolver. Usually a dropped ball, unforced forward pass, stupid penalty or missed tackle

Coat of Paint – Unit of measurement to describe the distance between a goalpost and the ball struck from a place kick or drop goal attempt that misses the target. The only other unit in the measurement system is the Country Mile

Collapsed Scrum – When the pressure of up to 8,000 Newtons of force channelled through the shoulders of the front rows reaches breaking point and six heads plunge towards the earth. One of them will be blamed, probably unfairly

Collisions, The – Collective noun for the multiple moments of heavy impact in a game, often seen as a barometer of 'who wants it more'. If a team is winning the collisions across the park, putting themselves on the front foot and their opponents on the back, they are likely going to win

Colts – The bright-eyed, bushy-tailed ones at the club without the heavy strapping, cauliflower ears, sideways nose, scar tissue and hint of a limp

Competitor, He's a – *Euph.* The player who will stretch the laws to the limit to gain an advantage. If that involves lamping someone or rubbing an elbow into their eye socket, so be it

Concussion – The medical and legal threat that hangs like a dark cloud over the future of the game

Contact Sesh – Hard training in virtual match conditions broken down into various forms: Full Contact, Controlled Contact and Live Set-piece. Intense but short to minimise injury ahead of the upcoming match. See also **Beasting**

Context of the Game, In the – Utterly pointless phrase meaning roughly 'what's going on out there'.

Contracts – A source of perennial friction between

player and club

Corporate Boxes – The band of smoked windows running along the middle of the main stand housing businessmen and their mates, who know as much of rugby as they know of Chinese calligraphy. The 'Prawn Sandwich Brigade' – a term of abuse in football, an honorific amongst rugby casuals. (If it's in focaccia so much the better)

Cough – Losing possession, often in the tackle, when the ball pops forward like an unintentional gobbet of phlegm

Counter-rucking – When the team not in possession hammer into the melée, forcing their opponents off the ball and grapple for a **Turnover**

Crash Ball – When a player running onto the ball at speed, usually in a crowded and tight midfield, deliberately smashes into the defender rather than look for space to run around him

Crash Ball Centre – Usually the chunkier inside centre used as a battering ram to breach the defences, cause disruption and open up a gap for the others to pour through

Creeping Into The Game, Errors – Contagious condition often caused by the dominance or slight advantage of the opposition, leading to a downward spiral of performance quality. Common symptoms include dropped balls, missed passes, daft penalties, knock-ons, poor throws and timing of the lift in the lineout

Creeping Into Their Minds, A Bit of Doubt – Both cause and general symptom of the errors (See above)

Criticism, Scathing – Never mild, criticism is only worth handing out if it scathes. No rugby team has ever received a mild admonishment at half-time

Crouch… Bind… Set! – Referee's instructions to front rows at a scrum, updated in 2013 from 'Crouch, Touch, Engage!' to create a more controlled collision and reduce risk of injury

Crowd Will Tell You If This One Goes Through – The rising roar of the spectators when a place kick is sailing towards the posts. Or the deathly silence if it is heading wide

Crumbs – Scrappy morsels of possession

Crunched – The effect of an especially heavy tackle

Cuff, Off the – Improvised, spontaneous play, favoured by visionary and eccentric fly-halves, that breaks out of the structures laid down on the training ground and brings a gasp of surprise and joy from crowd and commentator

D

Dark Arts – Of sinister and illegal activity taking place out of sight in the ruck or maul

Dark Horses – In an international sport dominated by a small elite, rugby has a herd of dark horses that can threaten not to win a tournament but beat one of the thoroughbreds and knock them off their stride. *A.k.a.* **Scotland**

Dead Ball – When the ball has crossed the line along the rear of the try area and the life of the play is terminated

Dead Rubber – Final game in a three-match series of matches, usually a British Lions tour, when one side has won the first two contests, no one gives a shit any longer and there's only pride left to play for, and career-threatening injuries to sustain in a pointless cause. Depressing stuff, but better than the fight for 'Bronze' match at the World Cup

Debrief – Post-match gathering when the battered players sit cross-armed, eyes glazed, and the coaches tell them where it all went wrong and produce video evidence of their crimes and misdemeanours

Decision-making – Only ever 'poor.' You never hear 'Excellent decision-making!' Taken as read that a player's decision will be a good one.

Deck – i) The pitch ii) Lay someone out

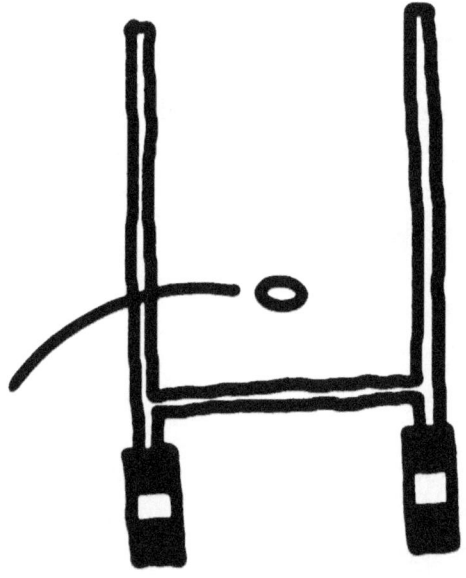

Dirt Trackers – The midweek team in a touring side obliged to take untarmacked roads to play remote

backwater teams

Dog, A Bit Of – *A.k.a.* A Bit of Mongrel. Of a player who enjoys the rough stuff, a bit of a scrap, usually a backrower showing his canine genes in the vicious dark arts of **Jackalling**

Donkey Work – The unglamorous graft carried out by the forwards in rucks and mauls that goes largely unnoticed by the spectators and commentators

Door Open, Left the – When a player has moved out of his default position, creating a gap for the opposition to exploit

Dot it Down – When there's plenty of time, not a defender in sight, to place the ball behind the try line

Drift Defence – The alternative to the Blitz Defence. When the defending backline drifts sideways across the pitch, shepherding the ball towards touch to pen it into a restricted area. Useful against teams with serious **Gas** on the wings

Drills – Tedious but important repetitive work on the training ground. Similar to soldiers square-bashing on the parade ground, the aim is to instil discipline, teamwork and precision so that, come the chaos of the fight, everyone is on automatic pilot

Droppie – *Aus.* Down Under slang for a drop goal

Dummy – When a player feigns to move one way, but goes the other, wrongfooting the defender. Rugby equivalent of offering a hand then putting the thumb to the nose and wiggling the fingers

Dummy Runner – Schoolboy-level decoy tactic where a player runs an obvious and hard line as if to receive the ball, only for the ball to be passed to someone completely

different, the idea being to sow doubt

Dump Tackle – When the tackler lifts his man off the ground and puts him backwards on his arse. Fun and kudos for the former, humiliation for the latter

E

Early Pressure – A period of time lasting roughly ten minutes when one team comes blasting out of the blocks, the other hangs on, before the match finally settles into its rhythm

Earning the Right to Go Wide – Curiously irritating expression, suggesting that running rugby is a moral issue embedded in some sort of UN Code of Human Rights and a team might find itself in a cage at The Hague if it flings the ball down the line without having put in the **Hard Yards**

Egg – The ball

Egg Chaser – Rugby player or fan

Eighty Minutes – You got to play all of them

Enforcer – The massive guy, usually a lock, with an inscrutable face, dark stubble and a monobrow who carries the air of a man who will beat you to a pulp if you so much as glance at his girlfriend or pint. One to avoid when the **Handbags** start wheeling

Engine Room – Usually of the two locks in the second row who pack down like a pair of hydraulic pistons in a steel works

Eye-Gouging – A hanging offence in rugby on a par of gravity with **Biting**. Surprisingly common in a gentleman's sport before the emergence of multi-cam TV coverage

F

Facial – *Euph.* Lovely expression for one player pressing or smearing the face of an opponent in the mud as he gets to his feet and trots off to the next ruck. Not a gallant act but not a grievous one either

Fairies – *Derog.* As defined by the forwards, the delicate, ethereal creatures of myth and fable with human features and gossamer wings, bearing a remarkable resemblance to the line of unmuddied and unbloodied backs strung out across the field behind them

Fallen Off, The Wheels Have – Playing on the metaphor of a team as a vehicle that has fallen to pieces in transit and ground to a halt

Fatties – *Derog.* As defined by the backs, the oafish lumps rolling around in the mud over the way while they peer into their compact make-up mirrors and wait to be handed the ball

Fend – More poetic way of describing a **Hand-off**

Few Beers – *Euph.* A massive, messy, post-match drinking session as described to the coach or wife

Fiery – *Dipl.* Of a hot-headed liability always getting carded and letting down his teammates

Fifty-fifty Ball – Ball is loose and up for grabs

Fill In – Street brawling jargon to describe a fist-beating when it all kicks off

Filthy – Of a master of the **Dark Arts**, usually a forward, probably a flanker, at ease with his conscience, handling in rucks, administering facials, standing on hands and ankles, rolling necks, holding players down etc

Fingers, how many am I holding? – First words a player might or might not hear after a heavy knock and sees the hazy figure of a man who looks remarkably like the team physio down on one knee before him

First Hit – Get it in early and hard, is the advice

First Receiver – Slightly jarring Americanism to describe the player to whom the scrumhalf passes the ball from a ruck or set piece. One of a number of quasi-scientific expressions creeping into the game giving the impression that rugby is more complicated than it is

Flat – i) When the defending backline have pushed right up to the off-side line ii) Horizontal pass iii) A match with lots of **Aerial Ping-Pong** and **Box Kicks**

Flat-footed – Of a player left rooted to the spot and the play passes him by in a rush

Fluids – Modern players don't take on water; they take on fluids

Flying Kick – When rugby turns into football and a player hacks the loose ball forward

Flying Wedge – *Arch.* Consigned, along with the **Cavalry Charge**, to rugby history in the drive to reduce the risk of serious injury, this involved a group of forwards, one of them with the ball, in a thundering advance from a penalty or free kick towards a thin static line. Deemed dangerous

Fold Up – Graphic description of what a heavy tackle to the midriff will do to a player, the head and boots jack-knifing together, the air expelled sharply from the lungs, the arse heading for the dirt, the ball anywhere

Forwards Win Games, Backs Decide By How Much – Like all clichés, this is a mildly irritating platitude with a kernel of truth in it

Foul Play – Any infringement of the laws or spirit of the game from high tackles and late hits to obstruction and deliberate knock-ons. There are as many ways to play foul as fair. See Also **Dark Arts**

Fourteen-pointer – An interception, runaway score when a try looked there for the taking at the other end. One minute, you've got seven points in the bag, the next you're seven worse off

Free Kick – The cheap version of penalty for a lesser offence from which you can neither score directly nor kick straight into touch to gain territory and earn a lineout. Not much choice but tap-and-go

French Flair – Romantic notion of Gallic glamour with ball in hand, free-flowing, inventive, risky rugby

Front Up – To deliver when it counts. See Also **Not A Backward Step**

G

Gain line – Imaginary line across the pitch running from the focus of the play – a ruck, maul or scrum. The aim, easier said than done, is to get beyond it and gain some territory

Game Awareness – Hazy phrase that sounds smart but doesn't mean much other than that a player is not a complete imbecile and knows roughly what he is meant to be doing

Game Plan – The cunning theory devised before the match that occasionally survives the first contact with the enemy and *their* game plan, and allows a team to impose itself

Gaps – An increasingly rare commodity against the highly-tuned defences of the modern game where space comes at a higher premium than Manhattan property opportunities

Garryowen – A very high, hanging kick. From the Limerick club of that name, the first team to use the high ball as a tactic. See Also **Up-and-Under, Bomb**

Gas – Speed. See Also **Wheels, Blistering Pace, Turbo**

Go North – When English players in the pre-professional era abandoned Union to switch codes to League, a paid sport, and headed up the M1 to the post-industrial heartlands of Lancashire and Yorkshire to earn a living from their skills rather than just play for the pints of beer and aftershave

Going Upstairs – Like phoning a friend for help on *Who Wants To Be A Millionaire?*, the match referee will turn to his TMO mate (Television Match Official) with all the screens up in a dark box in the stands to adjudicate on a tight decision he missed with his eyes

Good Head On His Shoulders – Sensible, solid lad who can be relied upon not to make idiotic decisions

Goose Step – When the ball-carrier straightens a leg in mid-sprint to unbalance the oncoming tackler, a move perfected by Aussie winger David Campese and by SS stormtroopers on parade. A curious misnomer. Geese don't actually walk like that. *A.k.a.* High Step

Got the Wood On – *Aus.* Ugly expression meaning to have the advantage over an opponent. Origins uncertain but probably something to do with touching wood for good luck

Grab The Bull by The Horns – Vacuous cliché. If you want to pacify a bull, you grab it by the ring in its nose

Grandmother Rule – The controversial rule that allows a player, born and bred and having learned all his rugby in one country, to play for the one that his grandparents had fled two generations earlier and with which he has no other affinity or loyalty

Grannygate – Scandal in the early 2000s when several players, unable to make their own national sides, claimed false ancestral roots to play for Wales or Scotland

Greasy Ball – Less of an issue in the modern game with balls made from high-synthetic rubber and superior grip designs. Long gone are the days of the smooth leather ball that turned into a large soapy egg in a light drizzle

Great Characters of the Game, One of – Old-school aftershave-drinking prankster

Great Vision – Overused praise for a player who's looked up from his boots and spotted an opportunity

Ground the Ball – Moment when the player touches the ball down behind the try-line. Modern camera angles have revealed that players are not as successful in this action as they were in the past. See Also **Dot Down**

Group of Death – World Cup qualifying group made up of strong teams from which only two of them can progress to the knockout stages

Grubber – Low-bouncing, threaded kick to run on to behind the back line, skimming like a stone on water, awkward for the defender to gather. Effective way to exploit space, wrong-foot the defence and cause a bit of chaos near the try-line

Grudge Match – Most matches are grudge matches for one reason or another, but some are grudgier than others, especially those against England, the birthplace of rugby

Gumshield – Once a piece of rough acrylic, today more of an oral computer, analysing G-Force and head acceleration to protect against concussion

H

Hacking – Kicking the loose ball forward or into touch

Hail Mary Pass – Desperate sling of the ball to a teammate, anyone in the vague vicinity, as the final whistle beckons, defeat looms and caution must be cast to the wind

Haircuts, The – Forwards will tell you they can spot a back from 100 paces by his fancier hairdo

Haka – Weird little pre-match traditional dance routine involving tongues and waggling fingers performed by the New Zealand All Blacks

Handbags – *Euph.* Commentator's description, often an understatement, for any form of dust-up, from a bit of shoving and shirt-pulling through to an X-rated, all-in bar brawl with bloodshed, ripped kit and red cards

Handling Skills – The ability to catch a ball and pass it

Hand Off – Push the heel of the hand into the face of the tackler to, quite literally, keep him at arm's length. A legal slap in the face

Hand Up, Put His – *Fig.* Not literally. When a player puts in a top performance or series of them to show he deserves his selection for a higher level

Hang Time – Ugly expression for the length of time a kicked ball stays in the air

Hard to Watch – Of an ugly, dull game usually featuring an abundance of errors, a stream of penalties and **Aerial Ping Pong**

Heads-up Rugby – Thinking man's rugby when a player or team shows superior **Game Awareness**, using the brain as well as the brawn. See Also **Play Smart**

Heart on his Sleeve, Wears His – Making excuses for the impulsive, unstable but likeable player who has lost his head and found himself in trouble

Helter-skelter – Common description of the early minutes of a match with adrenaline levels off the scale, frenetic, inaccurate, riven with errors, loose balls and flying tackles

Hem, North/South – Two hemispheres, two cultures, one rivalry

High Risk, High Reward – Risky rugby emphasising attack over defence

High Shot – A dangerous and illegal tackle above the shoulders, difficult to avoid if the tackler is 6'8" and the 'tacklee' is 5'7" and appears around the corner at pace

High Tempo – Stuff's happening out there, and it's happening fast

Hoist – Kick the ball very high but a shortish distance so that you and your teammates can be there when it returns to earth. See Also **Garryowen**, **Up-and-Under**, **Box Kick**

Hoof – Put the ball anywhere, just get it out of the danger zone

Hooker – The most unenviable position on the field, usually a tubby little fella. Arms draped over the **Props**, the hooker is helpless as a force equivalent to a car crash is pressed through his neck and shoulders at every scrum. Little wonder they don't always throw straight at the lineout. See also **Human Cannonball**

Hospital Pass – A pass from your teammate you are obliged to catch and get buried in the same instant by the onrushing tackler.

Human Cannonball – A small ball of fat, muscle and gristle topped with a filthy headband that resembles an artillery projectile when taking the ball in full flight. See Also **Hooker**

IJK

Ice Bath – A mild form of post-match torture before the beers, with the gratification deferred to the next day. Helps reducing swelling and inflammation, flushes out the lesser waste products (and the larger ones if you are pranking the next one in) and speeds recovery from all those hits

Ice Pack – The rugby player's hot water bottle bringing comfort to an injured limb

Icing on the Cake – Superfluous try, often a fancy one, with victory already wrapped up, to top off a perfect day out and leave everyone humming and wreathed in smiles

Impact From the Bench – Measurement of the effect, positive or negative, that the replacements bring to the performance

In his tracks, Stopped him – A hit so thundering it arrests the momentum of the ball-carrier there and then

In on the Burst – When a player takes the ball at full pelt in the hope of breaking clear

Inch, Not Giving One – What rugby players like to think they do in the heat of the contest

Industrial rugby – The rugby equivalent of 'agricultural cricket', rough around the edges, no finesse, old-school primitive stuff but no less of a spectacle for the coarseness

Inside Pass – A can-opener of a pass, one back towards the field rather than towards the touchline, very effective with a player coming fast on the inside shoulder and the defence drifting wide, exploiting the space left behind and opening a world of new opportunities

Inside-Out Pass – Actually two passes, and a deadly attacking weapon, the first pass in from the touchline to see off the tackler, and then the return pass with the coast clear

Interception – The dramatic moment when the team in the ascendancy, slinging the ball down the line, turns to see an opponent haring off in the opposite direction and bellyflopping under the posts. Blink, and you've missed it. See Also **Fourteen-pointer**

Jackal – *Noun or verb.* Scavenger for the ball, living off the scraps

Jersey, The – A team fights for the 'the jersey' as a regiment fights for 'the colours', whether it's country, professional club, junior rugby or the Brickhouse Gasworks 3rd XV

Keep Hold of the Ball – Tedious and obvious imperative like Please Shut the Gate in a field of bulls, No Smoking at a petrol station or hospital, or Do Not Feed the Crocodiles on a safari

Kick Tennis – When the full-backs decide to kick the ball to one another for a period, and the 28 players in between trot back and forth under its flightpath cursing and rolling their eyes. Rugby viewing at its lowest. See Also **Aerial Ping Pong**

Kicking Tee – A small rubber or plastic stand used for place kicks, not to be mistaken for the mouth guard

Knocking on the Door – i) Of a player putting in consistently impressive performances to warrant promotion ii) Actually knocking on a door

Knocks – Minor injuries carried by almost every player often concealed so they are not rested from the team

Knock-On – Spilling the ball forward and giving away a scrum

Knows the Way to the Try-line – Lame expression to describe a player who scores a lot of tries. You'd have to be pretty thick, or very concussed, to have to ask the way

L

Latcher – i) Player binding himself to the ball-carrier to add his power and weight to the momentum ii) The **Nause** following you around in the pub hoping to get in on the social

Late Tackle – One of rugby's deadly sins, considered dangerous, punishable by a penalty if mildly late, a yellow card if very late, and by a red card if the main camera has already swung away

Lateral, Playing a Bit – Fancy way of saying a team is gaining no ground

Laying the Platform – Steady start to a game, establishing control, securing clean ball, winning the collisions, maybe sinking a penalty or two

Lawmakers – A mystical cabal of nameless men, never seen in public, constantly tinkering and adjusting the laws of the game in order to piss off, blindside and confuse coaches, players and fans

Leadership – Indefinable quality of natural authority, expressed in words and/or actions, often found in the captain, that will inspire, guide, even scare a team to higher performance, and provide a rallying point around which a team can unite and bond

Leadership Group – When you can't see the players for the skippers. The modern phenomenon of encouraging a number of players, either senior ones or playing in key positions, to share the captain's burden. Like a military junta

Left Nothing in the Tank – Fuel storage metaphor describing a team or player that has expended every last drop of effort in the cause as they leave the field but not so fast that they are left **Running on Empty**

Leg Speed – Pompous phrase that has kneed 'acceleration' out of the lexicon

Lifting – Two players, front and back, assisting the jumper to reach the lineout throw, raising him to about 15 feet, high enough to feed a handful of leaves to a mature giraffe

Like another Loose Forward – Describing a jackal-like back, showing off to the **Fatties**, loving the loose ball and the breakdown play

Line Speed – The rate at which the defending backs advance using **Blitz Defence**. It only works if the rate is high

Lineout Call – Encoded in a secret cipher like 'Top Banana 666!', this is the shoutout before the throw-in to identify the lineout jumper to receive the ball and the subsequent move, if any, to follow. Once, always the hooker's call, at elite level today, it is more likely to be the 'lineout leader' calling the shots

Lions Tour – Four-yearly rugby spectacular when an elite squad of players from England, Ireland, Wales and Scotland take on one of the three giants of the Southern Hemisphere in a tour and Test series. Source of profound excitement for the fan occasioning joy or despair in roughly equal measure

Little Things Right, Do the – A winning performance will be the aggregate of well-executed details, the sum of the small parts

Lock – Massive lad resembling Chewbacca from *Star Wars*, or Jaws from *The Spy Who Loved Me*, tasked with jumping high at the lineout, pushing hard at the scrum and throwing his weight about in the loose. *A.k.a.* Second rower

Lock Horns – Tired but surprisingly accurate metaphor for the clash of two packs. As in the rugby season, so in the rutting season when stags lose 30 percent of their bodyweight, the testosterone levels soar, they become aggressive and territorial, they roar threats, they strut and posture to show off their strength, they roll around in mud and urine, and then they fight

Loosehead – The prop with his head visible on the side of the scrum whose main job is to destabilise the opposing **Tighthead**, the one with the power and technique to cause the damage and determine the fate of the engagement

Loose Carry – Phrase borrowed from rugby league referring to the failure of the player to hold the ball securely, making it vulnerable to being knocked clear or **Stripped**. An area of the game that has triggered legal confusion and controversy. See Also **Ball Security**

Lovely Hands – When a player displays exceptional handling skills (soft pass, quick release, crafty pop-up etc)

Lump, Big – Term of endearment for an especially large player

M

Made to Look Silly – Of a player left groping at the air or parked on his arse after some magic by his opponent

Mark – Deflating moment when play stops after a high ball is gathered in the defenders' 22-metre area, usually by the full-back, he raises a limp fist and mutters, 'Mark', wins the free kick and boots it back downfield or into touch. See Also **Bread Basket**

Master of his Trade – It's tough for commentators in the heat of the broadcast, but this is unacceptable doggerel

Maul – i) A wrestle for the ball involving at least three players, generally about ten, performed standing up rather than writhing in the mud ii) Any newspaper headline involving Leicester Tigers

Meat Pie – *Aus.* Rhyming slang for try

Meat Grinder – Attritional battle between the forwards, each set seeking to make mincemeat of the other

Meathead – *Derog.* Big, tough and stupid

Meat Wagon – An electric medical cart sometimes used to transfer stretchered players from the field in the case of grave injury

Medical Joker – Expression from French club rugby for a player signed short-term as an injury replacement. Refers to the playing card, not the badinage skills of the player signed

Men to Burn – When there are so many men to pass to in the attacking line, you could remove most of them, tie them to the stake on a big pyre and set fire to them. See Also **Overlap**

Mental Shape and Fitness – Once an area of player conditioning openly ridiculed and associated with feebleness, it took almost 150 years to acknowledge that belief, confidence, focus and resilience are as important to performance as press-ups and running at tackle bags. No one laughs at the sports psychologist today

Mental Toughness – The fruit of good mental fitness

Mercurial – Shit one week, great the next. Often said of French teams over the years. *Which one will turn up?*

Midweek Game – When the **Dirt Trackers** on a touring side take to a one-horse town in the backwoods looking to keep up the momentum and morale, and put their name forward for a Test spot with a good display

Milking – Ugly little development borrowed from football when a player points to an infringement, telling the ref to do his job, in the hope of a penalty. If the game ever witnesses players writhing on the floor feigning injury, it's all over

Mind Games – Low-level psy-ops, usually a media story rather than a reality, when a coach says something about the opposition ahead of a big clash. The comments tend to be flattering not critical, leading to the suspicion of skulduggery and leading the opponents into false sense of complacency

Miracle Ball – An outstanding pass delivered under extreme pressure, in the tightest of situations or that no one can have foreseen

Mismatch – Of a World Cup group game between, say, New Zealand and Pitcairn Island or Tristan de Cunha

Mix the Game up – Tactics as Liquorice Allsorts: a grubber, a box kick, a back row move, a throw to the back of the lineout, a coconut roll, a jelly button, a domed fondant…

Momentum – Mystical property gained by a team that has edged into the ascendancy by winning the small battles

Muckers – Borderline homo-erotic friendship between two besties in a team who always get changed at neighbouring pegs, shampoo each other in the showers and braid each other's armpit hair

Mulligrubber – *Aus.* Poetic Aussie form of **Grubber**, a low, skidding kick behind the lines

N

Nause – Irritating, over-eager character outside of the team trying to ingratiate himself and get down with the cool guys

Need to Stand Up – (…and be counted) Moral instruction for a team not 'fronting up' or 'stepping up to the plate'

Niggle – The first signs of trouble brewing, **Handbags** soon to be drawn and wheeled

No-Look Reverse Pass – About as cool and classy as it gets, when a player shapes to pass one way then flicks the ball the other way behind the back or across the body, never looking at the receiver. High risk. Looks dumb if the ball just drops to the ground

No More Than They Deserve – Cliché but no other way of saying it

Non-Travelling Reserve – You're not good enough to make the squad for the tour, but you can't go on holiday or make plans either, so it's a month or two in purgatory discreetly praying someone gets injured, but not too badly

Not A Backward Step – Tough-guy talk, going toe-to-toe with the opposition

Not Straight – Low moment for the hooker when his pissed throw-in sways off course and hands the lineout, or a scrum, to the opposition, puncturing hopes and reversing momentum

Not That Sort of Player – When the quiet, retiring lad

goes psycho, lamps someone, gouges an eye or stamps on a face

Nudge – Slang understatement for a place-kick

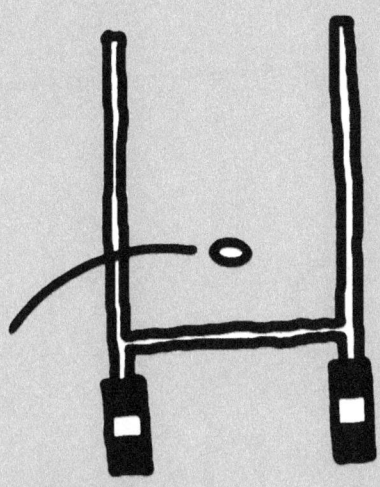

Numbers! – A cry of hope and joy when there's **Men to Burn** and the try is on

O

Obstruction – Pretending to mind your own business – *what me?* – but slyly blocking an opponent getting to the ball or ball-carrier

Off the Bench – When the bright-eyed, bushy-tailed, fresh-legged lad who has been **Riding The Pine** for 60 minutes bounces into the action in his lovely clean kit

Off-feet – **Pingable** offence at the breakdown when caught playing the ball on the ground, the feet are not rooted to the turf and a master of the **Dark Arts** will get to work in the melée

Offload, Lovely little – A diet pass. Cute pop-up by a player as he is buried in the tackle

On the Brink of Something Special – Of a team who has won half a dozen games on the trot and has a couple of promising youngsters coming through

On the Full – Like the **Not Straight** throw, a deflating moment when a hand-kick from anywhere other than within the player's 22-metre line goes into touch without bouncing on the pitch, killing momentum and handing the **Oppo** a lineout from where he kicked

Openside – i) The broad side of the playing area at a scrum or breakdown ii) The faster of the two flankers on that side of the scrum. See also **Blindside**.

Oppo, The – *Abbrev.* The fifteen men opposite

Out of the Blocks – The team's response to the first whistle. 'Quick' good, 'slow' bad

Over the Top – Technical term describing **Pingable** act of illegal entry at the breakdown, flying into a ruck over the ball rather than binding on

Overlap – When the attacking team has more players than the defenders and a try looks on. See Also **Numbers!**, **Men to Burn**

Ownership, Taking – Ugly buzz phrase that has crept out of business self-management jargon, meaning roughly, step up and act like it's yours

P

Pack – An accurate word, around since the late 19th century, to describe the eight forwards, a mob of highly aggressive predators and scavengers, working as a unit out on the hunt and going in for the kill

Pack Down – When the three rows of the scrum set and bind themselves, and prepare to engage the opposing pack

Paddock, The – Always 'the' never 'a', this refers to the pitch in current use

Panic Stations – When a heavily losing team looks up at the scoreboard and has not the first clue how to work their way back into contention

Pen – *i) Abbrev.* Penalty ii) Restrict a team or a player to a small area of the pitch

Percentage Rugby – *Euph.* Extremely dull, cautious rugby when the ball is rarely passed beyond the fly-half

Phases – Units of action performed by the attacking side between blasts of the whistle

Physical Battle – Almost meaningless quasi-tautological phrase to describe the physical battle that is a game of rugby

Piano Movers – The forwards who do the heavy lifting so that the backs get to play a few pretty tunes

Picked off his Laces – When the player gathers a pass heading for the dirt, usually moving at speed

Pilfer – The act of nicking the ball and turning over possession at the breakdown. See Also **Jackal**, **Poacher**

Pill – Slang for ball

Pill-Smasher – Perennially injured or hypochondriac player constantly hoovering anti-inflammatories and mineral supplements

Ping – Verb for penalise

Pint & Pie Rugby – Honest no-nonsense amateur game in which punches are thrown during the game and hearty beer tricks are performed afterwards in the clubhouse over a pie, if they're lucky, but more likely cheap sausages and cold chips

Plan B – When Plan A turns out to have been a shit idea

Playing the Percentages – Safe play, no risks, territory before possession, short and tight passing, kicking for touch, taking the three points over gambling on a try

Possession is 9/10ths of the Law – A truth in rugby as much as in Law where possession does not grant ownership but does give a significant advantage to the claim. The ball is yours until it is stolen back

Placer – Poor sod who has to lie down in the dirt on a windy day and hold the top of the ball for the kicker to stop it blowing over and risk having his hand booted between the posts

Play Smart – Using the brain as much the brawn. See Also **Heads-Up Rugby**

Player Escort – Unpaid minor, about ten-years-old, who gets to walk out next to a player and make sure he behaves himself in the tunnel before the anthems

Poacher – Usually of a scavenging flanker nicking the ball back at the breakdown. See Also **Pilfer, Jackal**

Pocket – According to the forwards, a small pouch sewn inside the shorts so that the backs have somewhere to keep their make-up

Pocket, In the – A small parcel of land in a perfect location occupied by the fly-half readying himself for the drop-goal or clearance from the try line

Pop Kick – Cute little dink over the defender, like a **Chip** but shorter, a matter of yards, played with the view to gathering it on the full

Pops a Pass – Neither a full pass nor a dinky offload

Post-Match Drinking Session – Long-standing rugby tradition as old as the game, vital for team bonding and upsetting the spouse or partner; a gateway activity leading to nightclubs, police cells and a morning appearance before the magistrate. See Also **Few Beers**

Postman – The place-kicker who always delivers under pressure

PowerPoint Slide Presentation – Tedious two-hour session in an uncomfortable chair with arms folded, pre – or post-match, watching the coach use a stick to point at maps of the London Underground showing lines and positions and some miniature writing

Preparation, Our – ... For the game was excellent... I don't know what went wrong

Professional Foul – Deliberate infringement with degrees of gravity, inviting any of the punishments on offer from a mere penalty to dismissal from the field

Prop – One of the two Captain Pugwash lookalike competition candidates holding up the little tubster in the middle

Pub Team – *Derog.* i) A very poor team ii) A team from a pub

Pudding, Bit of a – A slow, heavy player lacking agility, usually a **Prop**

Pulling The Strings Out There – Playing on the metaphor of the fly-half as puppeteer controlling the movement and drama of the spectacle

Pushover – A try scored when the scrum shoves the opposition back over the try line and the Number Eight touches down

Put Head in the Spokes – Brave, borderline insane tackle at a moment of crisis when the player torpedoes low and hard towards the ball-carrier's spinning boots in order to bring him down as sharply as possible

Pylons – The towering lineout jumpers, usually the two **Locks**

Quality Ball – Consistency in the ball being delivered tidily and efficiently from the breakdown or set-piece. See Also **Clean Ball**

Quick Throw – An off-the-cuff lineout when one player lobs the ball to a teammate to catch a team off-guard or out of position. Increasingly rare sight in modern rugby owing to improvements in defensive organisation with players less likely to be scattered all over the pitch like the Battle of Towton (1461)

R

Raking – Underhand accidental practice of scraping the studs over an opponent on the ground in trying to retrieve the ball from a ruck

Real Estate – Wide open spaces ripe for development

Recovery Drinks – i) Rehydrating isotonic drinks

packed with electrolytes and minerals ii) A **Few Beers** after the match

Red Card – The ultimate sanction for foul play with the poor consolation of the showers all to yourself to reflect on your stupidity or recklessness

Red Zone – Coach jargon to describe the opposition's area between the 22-metre mark and the try line in a more exciting way

Regroup – Usually an activity that takes place at halftime after a first-half mauling characterised by low-hanging heads and fierce advice from the coach

Rehab – The period of purgatory between injury and playing again

Retaliation, Got it in First – Taking someone out before they lay you out

Reverse Pass – Cool trick when a player shapes to pass one way but switches or slips it the other way, behind his back if he's feeling very bold. See Also **No-Look Reverse Pass**

Reverse Treadmilling – Walking or running against the flow of the rubber belt for a tougher workout challenging strength, balance and muscle memory. Used in **Rehab**, it's becoming an everyday gym routine

Riding the Pine – The men saddled up on the replacements' bench or in **the Sin Bin**

Right Areas, Play in the – Stupid way of saying the opposition's 22-metre area

Roll of the Dice – Always final. No one rolls the dice in the middle of a match

Rolling Maul – Excellent name for a heavy metal band describing the pack on its feet, moving forward as a unit, sliding each other the ball to change the point of momentum

Round-the-Corner Kicking – When the place kicker comes at the ball from the side rather than straight at it: three or four steps back, two or three to the side, always looking at the ball in case they forget where they put it

Ruck – i) Loads of guys rolling around the ground and wrestling each other in the hunt for an egg-shaped ball

ii) A punch-up

Rugby Gods – Fickle divine beings with an interest in the oval-ball game, prone to favouritism, bestowing gifts and good fortune on one team, plagues and pestilence on the other

Rule Changes – Porn for lawyers and administrators messing around with the Do's and Don'ts of the game. See Also **Lawmakers**

Run With the Ball, Loves to – Dogs love fetching sticks too. Nonsense expression. What player doesn't?

Runners – Any number of attacking players taking off on different lines and angles to confuse the defence as the ball is about to be delivered

Running Game – Attacking, free-flowing rugby bringing the backs into constant play, the opposite of **Percentage Rugby**

Running On Empty – When a player or team has given everything to the cause but there's nothing left in the tank

Rush Defence – A lighter version of **Blitz Defence** in which most of the defensive line surge towards the attackers to cut down time and space and force errors

S

Schoolboy Mistakes – Using junior players as the gold standard of failure. How encouraged they must be to hear themselves cited as the benchmark of uselessness!

Scotland – Small, dark country to the north of England with about 27 players to choose from, most of them imported under the Grandmother Rule, managing somehow still to compete at international level

Scotland's Year, This could be – Tired old phrase rolled out by pundits every year, around Burns Night, ahead of the Six Nations to make the tournament seem wide open and fire up extra interest amongst the punters

Scrummie – *S Hem*. Endearing moniker for the dinky little half-back behind the pack

Scud Missile – Ferocious tackle at speed rocketing out of a clear blue sky

Senior Players – The Firm. Self-appointed caucus of half a dozen wizened and wise players who everyone else in the squad must respect and obey or find themselves in the reserves

Sesh – i) Training session ii) See Also **Few Beers**

Shamateurism – Before the professional era began in 1995 when the best amateur players played for the sheer love of the game, very generous 'expenses' for kit and travel, and enjoyed comfortable office jobs with as much 'leave' as they liked

Sheds – The changing rooms

Shoe Pie, Shoeing/Bit of a – *Euph*. Stamping, kicking or raking a player. Other treatments in the scrum spa package include a facial, eye makeover, exfoliation and excess hair removal

Short Arm – A free kick signalled by the referee with a bent arm rather than a raised one for a full penalty

Shove on, Get the – When the scrummagers find their feet and a harmony of power to jerk back the opposing pack

Shut the Gate – i) When a team has built up a decent

lead and sets about protecting it by reining in the attacks and concentrating on protecting their patch ii) Close a gap in the defensive line

Siege Mentality – What a squad claims to enjoy when, encircled and battered by critics and haters, they hole up in camp and plot their counterattack to see them off

Slowing Down – Effort to prevent the opposition recycling the ball quickly. Legal ploys include getting over the ball after the tackle, counter-rucking, rolling the player and the **Choke Tackle**

Snotter – A bone-shuddering tackle that forces mucus to shoot from the nose

Something to the Table, Bring – Lame cliché for making an impact

Spear Tackle – Hideous tackle punishable by a red card, lifting a player upside down off his feet, and spearing him into the turf by the head or neck

Stationary Bikes – Comic sideshow on the touchline when replacements, wearing long padded dressing gowns if it's cold, spin the wheels to get the blood up

Steamroller – A large ball-carrier ploughing straight over a hapless defender

Step – Short for side-step when a player shapes in one

direction only to step off in the other. Works every time

Sin Bin – The Naughty Step or Dunce's Corner where

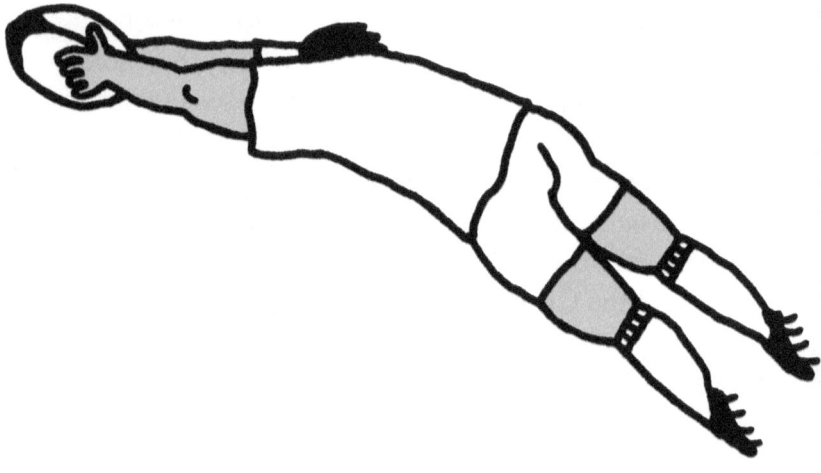

players shown a yellow card sit
for ten minutes to reflect on their foolishness before
being allowed to rejoin the class

Skip Pass – One that misses out the next player or two
in the attacking line

Snow on It, Coming Down With – Phrase wearied by
overuse to describe a ball that has been kicked very high.
No rugby ball has ever returned to earth covered in
hexagonal ice crystals, even when it's snowing

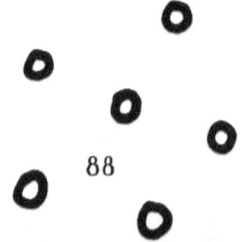

Soft Hands – Delicate handling skills under a pressure, taking and delivering a tight pass in an apparently effortless manner. See Also **Lovely Hands**

Spill – Drop the pill

Spine – Supposedly describing the key players in a line-up, the vertebrae being hooker, number eight, scrumhalf, fly-half and full-back. 'Brain' would be more accurate than spine, these positions being more those of the principal decision-makers than structural elements

Spiral Pass – A long-distance spinning pass with the same aerodynamic properties as a bullet or a quarterback's pass, offering speed and accuracy of delivery

Spray – An adventurous kick or pass over a longer distance

Squeaky Bum Time – Tight finish, high hopes riding on the result, and everyone's wiggling in their tiny plastic seats with tension and excitement

Stats, The – Once a matter of how many points are shown on the board and how many beers drunk after, today a full carnival of data systems and microscopic analysis into the smallest areas of performance, some of it useful

Steal – … space that isn't obvious, or the ball at the

breakdown, the lineout throw from the attacking side, the momentum by slowing down play …

Stick the Ball up Your Jumper, Just Need to – Old-timer's call to f**k the data and the fancy jargon and go back to how the game used to be played in the good old days

Stomping – Assaulting prone player with boot and stud. More common in **Pint & Pie Rugby** but rarely seen in a televised game

Strapping – Heavy bandaging, the unofficial kit supplements worn by older battle-scarred players, taped to legs and arms to stop them coming loose and falling off

Strength in Depth – Of a large, high-quality squad, a phrase usually heard when the **Bomb Squad** comes off the bench and stands in an imposing phalanx on the

touchline ready to do battle

Strip– Rip the ball from its carrier

Structured Rugby – Pre-planned rugby, sticking to the game plan, discouraging improvisation and spontaneity, the aim being to seize control of the game and hold it

Subs Suit – Hideous item of sports fashion, like a shit XXXL dressing gown, that replacements peel off before mounting the stationary bikes to look even more ridiculous

Super Slow Motion – A technological innovation to make an infringement look way worse than the reality, the home crowd adding their groans and gasps to influence the referee and get him to brandish the cards

Suspension – The sentence for a hanging offence e.g. a spear tackle, punching, eye-gouging handed down by a panel of wise men with white hair

Swarming Defence – Like a street mugging, when more than one player rushes the ball carrier

T

Tackle Suit – Cartoon superhero costume with garishly coloured foam pads sported by the **Bin Juice** during training

Take Out – Hitman job on a key player, sometimes legal

Take the Positives, We'll – … and move on. Meaningless captain's platitude after seeing his team pulled part, minced and buried

Take the Three – Going for the safe points at a penalty rather than gambling on a try

Tap & Go – When the scrum-half scents glory and takes off as soon as the penalty is awarded, often only to be marmalized by the gang of forwards standing in his way, or called back by the ref

Tap Tackle – A last-ditch, dramatic moment when the attacking player is clean through, but a flying dive and a fingertip to the ankle saves the day

TCUP–Swarming Defence

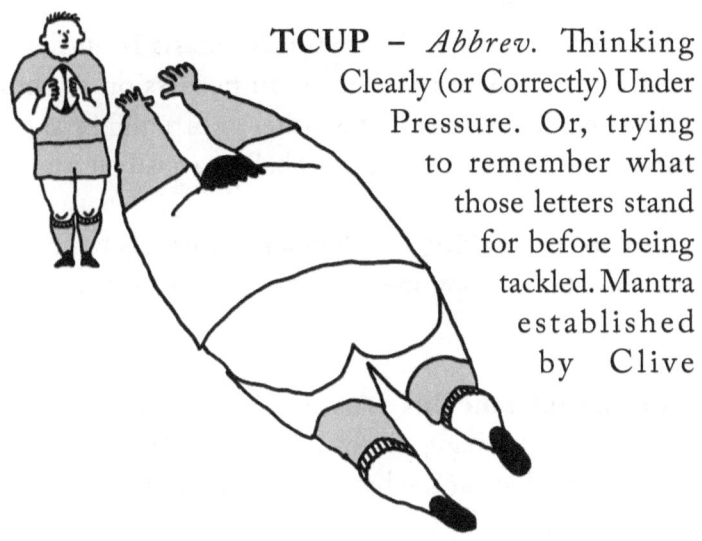

TCUP – *Abbrev.* Thinking Clearly (or Correctly) Under Pressure. Or, trying to remember what those letters stand for before being tackled. Mantra established by Clive Woodward with World Cup-winning England side

Team Bus – Long vehicle for multiple passengers carrying the away team to the stadium and inviting a flying headbutt when England pull into Cardiff. Fact: they headbutt buses in Wales

Team Social – See **Few Beers, Post-Match Drinking Session**

Ten in the Bin, That's – Gut reaction of the commentator predicting a yellow card when a player fouls up badly

Ten-man Rugby – Tight, defensive, kicking rugby, the ball prohibited from passing the fly-half, and the rest of the backline are on tackle and chasing duty for the day

Territorial Game – When the emphasis is on field position and kicking rather than possession of the ball, often deployed in bad weather or in a high-stakes game, lowering the risk of a wet ball or a costly mistake

There for the Taking – When a team has its boot on the throat of its opponents and it's time for the *coup de grace*

Thrown Under the Bus – An unwelcome situation generated by a teammate, usually a **Hospital Pass**, or being left to go it alone at the breakdown or exposed in wide open spaces

Tight Head – The prop with his head inside the scrum who – whisper it around the **Loosehead** – is the more technically demanding and important role of the two

Tins – *S Hem.* A player with handling skills so poor he might as well have tins for hands

TMO – Television Match Official: Sinister, powerful character somewhere in the bowels of the stands, fickle purveyor of joy and despair, invited by the craven referee to make the tough call on a close try or an act of foul play

Toe Punt – Ugly boot of the ball with the end of the

foot, usually in desperation to clear a loose ball into touch near the tryline

Togetherness – Soft, modern, jargony word for team or squad unity

Torpedo – i) *A.k.a.* spiral punt that, spinning fast by kicking a little across the middle of the ball, achieves greater distance and **Hang Time** ii) Dodgy no-arms tackle leading to cards

Touch – The area beyond the field of play

Touch Judge – Eager little chap with a colourful flag haring up and down the side of the pitch trying to observe the play without tripping up or running into an advertising hoarding

Tourist, Great – Dirt-tracker for the midweek games unlikely to feature in the Tests, but a morale-boosting laugh in the bar, full of japes and high spirits, dive-bombing the pool and filling boots with shaving foam and turds

Train the House Down – Train hard and well. See Also **Beasting Session**

Travel Well, French Teams Don't – Unbeatable within

the sound range of their own church bells, Gallic teams, like fine wines, supposedly don't go down so well on the road

Treatment – i) Official: With physio or medic, on or off the pitch. ii) Unofficial: See **Facial**

Trolleyed – When a player is wiped out in a tackle and may need a gurney to remove him from the pitch

Truck And Trailer – A rolling maul with loads of players hanging off the back behind the ball-carrier

True Rugby Man – Someone with no life or interests outside the game

Tuba in the Strings Section – Big lad, usually a prop, who finds himself amongst the prancing divas in the backline at a critical moment in the performance, triggering a deep bass groan from the crowd

Tunnel – The dark passage between the two locks through which the hooker once backheeled the ball to the number eight at a scrum

Turbo, Turned on the – When the ball-carrier fleeing towards the try-line goes up an extra gear to get clear of his pursuers. See Also **Wheels, Gas, Blistering Pace**

Turnover – Precious ball won back from the opposition, restoring possession, switching the momentum and striking a psychological blow

Turnstile Defence – When attacking players spin through the defenders like it's rush hour at Waterloo Station

U V

Uncontested Scrum – Miserable spectacle when, for safety reasons, two packs are obliged to engage as though the others were a collection of Ming vases because one side has lost its front row players to injury or cards

Under the Pump – *S Hem*. When a team is under extreme duress. Origins of word probably nautical, working the bilge pump to prevent the boat from sinking

Under the Opponents' Skin – Winding up the other side with chirping banter, sly fouls, mischief at the breakdown, a lucky break or two, slowing down the ball, ruffling hair, patting bottoms

Up-and-Under – A high kick to chase. See Also

Garryowen

Upsetting the Chemistry – Bringing on a player inappropriate for the match conditions or disrupting a team in good flow

Use it or Lose it – Referee's barking command to a team to get a move on and do something with the ball at a maul or risk possession being handed over

Under the Sticks – A kick or field position right below the posts

Unceremoniously Dumped – Curiously common expression for a heavy tackle. When has a player ever been neatly and politely placed on his backside?

Unstoppable – Of a very powerful player who has gone over for a try from close range

Using the Full 23 – Making the most of every fresh leg available amongst the eight replacements

Variation – Mixing up the tactics and angles of attack

Varsity Match – When Oxbridge graduates take time off from punting and sleeping in lecture halls to watch their Light & Dark blue representatives knock lumps out of each other at Twickenham and everyone gets frightfully tipsy

WXYZ

Wales – Great rugby nation currently enfeebled by the modern love of football, the demise of mining communities and poor administration

Wanted It More, They – Usually unfounded criticism of a team that has given its all but happened to come out second best against a better team on the day

Washing Machine – A chaotic breakdown where bodies are flying everywhere

Webb Ellis, William – Victorian-era origin myth of a rebellious boy at Rugby School, bored with football, picking up the ball and running up field, giving birth to the game of Rugby. The substantial kernel of truth in the fable is that the school was the first institution to lay down a set of rules

Wheeling – When the scrum rotates more than 90 degrees. If naturally, the ref will reset it. If illegally, because one pack is trying to stop clean ball, there will be a penalty

Which Team Will Turn Up? – Of a wildly inconsistent side, commonly said of the French over the years, brilliant one week, awful the next

White Boots – Vogue fashion creeping into the game, especially in the southern hemisphere, fancied more by frilly-footed backs in the northern but largely shunned by the harder types in the front five preferring an honest old-fashioned black boot

Win the Collisions – To dominate the moment of contact in attack or defence. Win more of them than you lose and the game is yours

Win Ugly – Forget the fancy stuff; just get the W in the scorebooks by any means, no matter how dull or unattractive the manner

Winning Games they're not Supposed to Win – Of a good side not playing well but somehow a core of quality and doggedness keeps getting them over the line

Wonderful Servant – Like a long-serving footman or scullery maid, the long-serving player will never be forgotten in his rugby mansion

Won't Die Wondering – Giving it everything so that there can be no regrets

Works Team – *Derog.* Poor performance likened to that of a team of casuals from the steelworks. See also **Pub Team**

Wheels, Got – Quick as a getaway car. See Also **Blistering Pace, Gas, Turbo**

X-Rated– Of an especially brutal match or act of foul play

Yards, Hard – *Aus. A.k.a.* Hard Yakka. Borrowed from rugby league to describe the dogged physical effort, especially in the early stages, that creates the platform from which the game can be won

Zinzan – Distant, implausible drop-goal effort by a forward who has lost his mind. Named for All Black great Zinzan Brooke who managed three drop goals in Tests

Acknowledgements

Peace, love and happiness to Mudd Bexley for her brilliant, funny illustrations and to Andrew and Rebecca Brown at Principal Publishing, as always too, for their slick and efficient design work on the covers and interior.

About the Author

Niall Edworthy is one of the UK's most prolific and successful ghostwriters and a best-selling author of non-fiction and fiction in his own right and under his own name. A former Sport and News reporter for broadsheet newspapers and the international wire agencies AFP and Reuters, he has covered the Olympics, World Cups and European Championships in several sports including the 1995 & 1999 Rugby World Cups.

Niall began writing books in 1997. His first book was *England: The Official FA History*, his second *Lord's: The Home of Cricket*, the third *The Second Most Important Job in the Country*, the story of England's managers and the trials they endured. One of the first books he ghosted was on behalf of a key player in England's 2003 World Cup winning side.

He is the author or ghost of almost 50 titles, most for the big publishing houses, many of them for well-known names (actors, soldiers, musicians, sportsmen & television personalities), others for 'ordinary' people with extraordinary stories. He has written in a wide range of genres, mainly Biography, History and Natural History but also Humour, Sport and recently, in Fiction. His first novel, *Otto Eckhart's Ordeal*, was shortlisted for the Wilbur Smith Best Published Novel Award 2021.

If you enjoyed Badger's Rugby Compendium, you might also enjoy *Badger's Football Slang and Banter*, *Badger's Cricket Compendium* and *Badger's Golf Compendium*, Jack Bremner's *Shit Ground No Fans*

NIALLEDWORTHY.COM

www.ingramcontent.com/pod-product-compliance
Lightning Source LLC
Chambersburg PA
CBHW020341010526
44119CB00048B/557